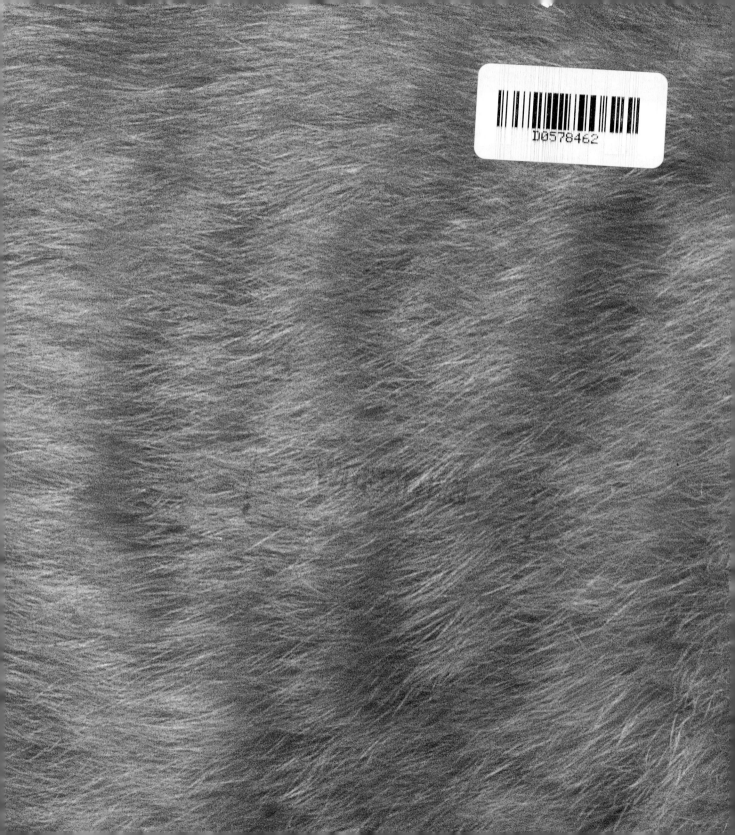

Cats into Everything

Holidays provide welcome opportunities for family, friends, and felines to come together. For Louise, her first Christmas was an eye-opening time to leap into the spirit of the season: tree climbing, package shredding, ornament swatting. . . .

The Cats' House
5010 Northaven Avenue
San Diego, California 92110-1116
(619) 276-3621

bobcat@thecatshouse.com
www.thecatshouse.com

99 00 01 02 03 TWP 10 9 8 7 6 5 4 3 2 1

Library of Congress Cataloging-in-Publication Data
Walker, Bob.
Cats into everything / Bob Walker.
p. cm.
ISBN 0-8362-6917-9 (hardcover)
1. Cats—California—San Diego—Anecdotes.
2. Cats—California—San Diego—Pictorial works.
3. Photography of cats. 4. Walker, Bob. I. Title.
SF445.5.W35   1999
636.8'0887—dc21
98-46312   CIP

Cats into Everything

Bob Walker

Andrews McMeel
Publishing

Kansas City

It was a good fire, although Frances and I didn't think so at the time. Like the mythical phoenix rising from life's ashes, we painstakingly rebuilt our framing/photo gallery and reopened with a gala party. It didn't take long for us to realize that we were tired of "going" to work and closed our store. That decision allowed us to work at home with our cats (and dog)—doing the same thing (for less)—and enjoy life's surprises more.

Living and working with a household full of felines has demonstrated what all cat lovers know: Cats will purr and play and carouse their way into all aspects of their feeders' lives. Whether we're working, eating, sleeping, or socializing—our cats are into everything we do.

In Frances's and my twenty-five years of feline companionship, we've observed that cats have a natural need to climb to the top of curtains, cupboards, and bookcases. They love to look down on us. So, we constructed more than one hundred feet of elevated walkway to allow our felines to frolic overhead. Immediately, our fortunate felines and their cat-scaled jungle gym became upwardly mobile media stars—celebrity hosts to an international assortment of film and print crews; and headliners of their own award-winning book, *The Cats' House*, and Web site (www.thecatshouse.com).

While our fortunate felines luxuriate in their elevated lifestyle, Frances and I struggle to answer their fan mail: "I'm going to prison. Will you keep my cat?" "Does your house smell?" "I just got a kitten. Would you tell me everything you know about cats?" There have been so many wonderful letters that it has become impossible to reply to all of them.

Cats into Everything is our visual confessional—Frances's and my attempt to literally let our cats out of their bags. You won't discover all of life's answers here, but you will find answers to some of your fellow cat lovers' questions. And, you'll meet the Cats' House cats (and dog Sasha) who share the experiences of all of us. For our family, there's truly no place like home. Our lives have become inseparable.

BobCat

There's
No Place
Like
Hom

Our Feline Family

Eccentrics have lots of cats

Denise

Frank

Louise

Charlotte

Frances

Bernard

Frances has always been a cataholic, and blessed with good fashion sense. In an effort to make Edward, her orange tabby, more stylish, young Frances knitted a cat-sized wool cap and matching set of four booties (footwear not shown—quickly rejected). She's always had cats, even though she would be better without them. Thankfully, with modern medicine, Frances is able to have her allergies and kitties and breathe too.

We were a cat couple right from the start. Frances and I adopted our first feline, Beauregard, on our wedding night. Almost immediately, our insatiable fondness/weakness for kittens/cats set in. Now, Frances and I enjoy nine cat companions, and consider two felines just a "starter kit."

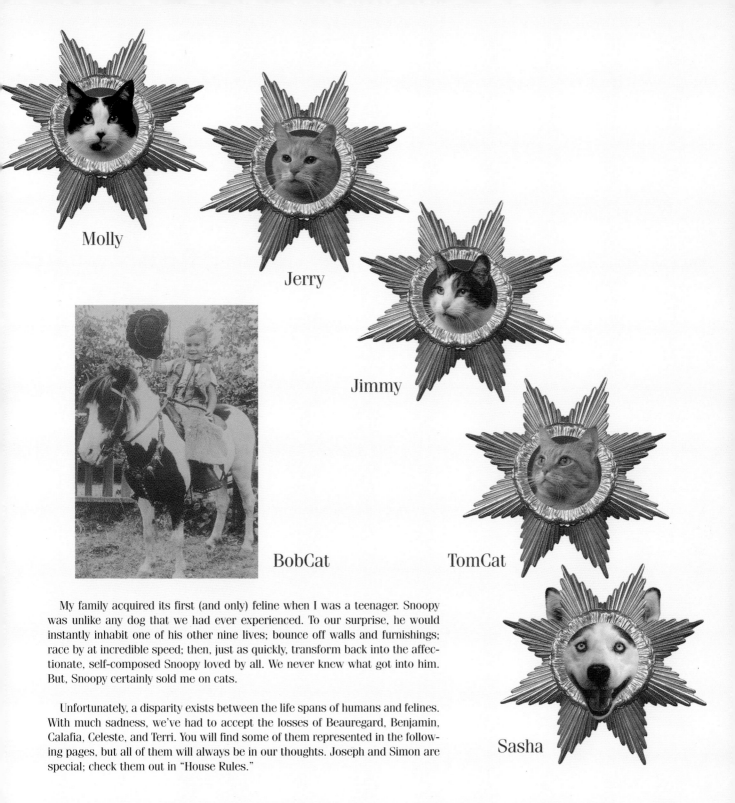

Molly

Jerry

Jimmy

TomCat

BobCat

Sasha

My family acquired its first (and only) feline when I was a teenager. Snoopy was unlike any dog that we had ever experienced. To our surprise, he would instantly inhabit one of his other nine lives; bounce off walls and furnishings; race by at incredible speed; then, just as quickly, transform back into the affectionate, self-composed Snoopy loved by all. We never knew what got into him. But, Snoopy certainly sold me on cats.

Unfortunately, a disparity exists between the life spans of humans and felines. With much sadness, we've had to accept the losses of Beauregard, Benjamin, Calafia, Celeste, and Terri. You will find some of them represented in the following pages, but all of them will always be in our thoughts. Joseph and Simon are special; check them out in "House Rules."

There's No Place Like Home

A New Kitten!

There comes a time in every cat lover's life when a new kitten is needed. For Frances and me, that irresistible urge to liven things up strikes more often than it does for most people, but, when it comes to cats, we know we're not normal. Thankfully, our feline family members do their best to support our urges.

"Everything was perfect until this thing arrived!" When our cats' arteries are getting a little sluggish, we introduce a new kitten. Almost immediately, their juices start flowing again. After the initial kitten shock, our formerly unruffled felines welcome their new roommate.

We all respond to change differently, and so do our cats. Under the cover of darkness (actually, through our garage door), Frances and I stealthily brought Molly, our newly adopted kitten, into the house. Our cats didn't have a clue that, just two rooms away, another feline was adjusting to her new surroundings. The next day, all emotions broke loose. We introduced each of our cats individually to Molly and captured their initial reactions. It is said that you can tell a lot about a person by how they react under stress. Obviously, cats are not people. Within a week, all of our family members were the best of friends!

Joseph

Frank

Jerry

Denise

Molly

TomCat

Bernard

Simon

Jimmy

There's No Place Like Home

April Fool's Dog

Our wildest dreams hadn't imagined this challenge to our cats' adaptability: Frances was loading groceries at the local supermarket when a wolflike dog leaped into our van. She had never experienced dogs before and was intimidated by this brazen Siberian Husky. What surprised me most was that Frances drove home with this scary creature jumping from seat to seat behind her. I, of course, said, "No, we can't keep her." Now, Sasha and I are best friends and can't imagine living without each other.

To find Sasha's owner, we advertised in the newspaper and placed her at the local shelter—both without success. Thankfully, adoption day arrived, and our Cats' House cats were rewarded with their own dog.

Cats
Are Not
Crows

Home is where our cats roam

One of the first things you'll notice when you share your space with a cat is that cats do not take direct routes. Crows may travel in a straight line, but every self-respecting cat knows that the shortest path is usually for the birds. It is far more fun to entertain everyone with nimble trailblazing up and over furniture, priceless heirlooms, and feeder's laps. How many people, while seated to read a good cat book, haven't been pricked by the needle-sharp claws of a feline that's "just walking through"? With this endearing feline trait in mind, Frances and I decided to make a few cat-friendly adjustments to our home.

Frank is not about to be caught traveling like a bird. He makes his own way to the swing.

Our Cats' House

Since our cats are always scanning and scheming for ways to get higher, we decided to elevate their lifestyle with a series of creative pathways for moving from room to room. A little home remodeling was the least we could do for them.

Four hundred feet of rope was wound around a floor-to-ceiling scratching post; huge cat-sized holes were cut in our walls; a spiral staircase and wall-to-wall ramp were constructed; and, to top it all off, over one hundred feet of elevated walkway was connected to create a room-to-room, seven-foot-high playground for our deserving companions.

Today, we're able to enjoy felines frolicking on our walls and overhead as they make their way throughout the house—but never in a straight line.

Our feline speedsters find it great fun to race up and down their spiral stair-case. The catwalk has become their complete activity center for game-play-ing, catnapping, observation, and sanctuary from children and other loud noises.

There's No Place Like Home

Through a flame-shaped opening, our elevated travelers enter their ruby red–illuminated hallway. Glowing neon guides the catwalkers in a zigzag path to our shared bedroom, the walkway's final destination.

Cats into Everything

Sixteen feet of carpeted ramp bring our aerial cats back to earth in our nightly-crowded bedroom. Many people ask, "Do you really sleep with nine cats?" Absolutely! They keep us warm in winter, and even warmer in summer.

There's No Place Like Home

Fur in Our Food

Probably the most important activity in the life of a cat is the capturing, playing with, and eating of food. For our felines, the "call of the wild" is the sound of the microwave timer alerting them that our meal is about to be served. They always act as if they are one meal away from starvation. Unfortunately for them, their ample girth betrays their plaintive meows.

Feeding Frenzy

The way our cats carry on at mealtime, we wouldn't be surprised to hear that cat food manufacturers secretly implant subliminal sounds into pop-top cans. Three times daily, the scene is the same: Pop the top of cat food and, immediately, we're surrounded by a swirling sea of tail-waving felines. All cat activities come to a screeching halt, naps are curtailed, and games stopped. There's no way that the manufacturers can claim our cats' frenetic reaction is because of their food. When meals are finally served, our pop-top zombies can be just as finicky as the next feline. No, cat feeders are not being told the truth: Pop-tops have irresistible catcalls embedded in them.

Mere cat food is no match for the fierce attack of a hungry feline. Denise devours her kibble with gusto.

Timeless Truths and Barbs

Cats are such fascinating creatures that they make you want to know more about their built-in features. For example: When they lick you, why is their tongue so scratchy? In my years of inquiry, I've discovered that there is no shortage of opinions.

"This is a young cat," the young boy announced after the cat licked his finger. "How can you tell?" I asked. "Cat's tongues get smoother as they get older. Their scratch wears off," he replied with authority. Not to be outdone, I provided one of my rarely voiced observations, "Another way of knowing the age of a cat is by counting the rings on their tail; the more rings, the older the cat." Both of us felt smug for being so well informed.

Cats are not alone in being curious. The first under-cat photos that I attempted were to document the barbs on their scratchy tongues. Barbs are important to cats. They allow them to lick the meat off of bones and penetrate their fur to keep it shiny clean.

Swarm Out, Swarm In

The favorite thing that our cats love to sink their barbs into is "people food." Unfortunately for them, our midday meals are eaten outside with Sasha. (Dogs need quality time too.) Plus, it's good for us as well: Fresh air, warm California sun, and in-your-lunch yellowjackets. When nature communes with us, we make a beeline for the calm of the indoors. "They've got chicken," TomCat probably meows. Because, as soon as we're inside, our plates are swarming with cats.

"Cats are independent." Sure. That might be what they would like us to think, but their actions suggest otherwise. For Frances's and my television viewing and meals, we all cluster in the TV room within a tight radius: Wherever we are (and our food is), they want to be too.

Cats into Everything

Not only do our cats get into the middle of our meals, they get involved in our TV viewing as well. Several years ago, we borrowed a television while ours was in for repair. Everything went berserk. All of our cats thought the new TV was great for napping on. But, without warning, it started turning itself on and off; channels changed erratically; and the volume went up and down. Apparently, when our slumbering felines were tossing and turning, they were activating the television's controls. Some product designer had placed all of the TV's "push-buttons" on top. Why? Everyone knows that cats are heat-seekers. We solved the problem by placing the television in a milk crate and stuffing books at its sides. Our CATV viewing became less exciting, but far more enjoyable.

People who are curious about our nine-cat lifestyle often ask: "Do they have their own food bowls?" Yes, and the ones next to them; and our plates too. If you want to see action (and out of plate experiences), come by at mealtime and view *Close Encounters of the Cat Kind*—the culinary thriller Spielberg could have made. Our cast of cats (and dog) is thoroughly seductive. Frances and I are no match for such talented actors. Generations of felines have passed down performance skills to prevent the starvation of their species. Rhythmic purrs, caressing body rubs, and tender expressions melt us in no time at all. And, if kindness fails, the direct approach is always available.

TomCat's lightning-fast reach and razor-sharp claws keep him well fed with our chicken.

Furtive
and *Fast*

Capturing chicken off a moving fork is a game easily mastered. And, beef is tasty (but there's no skill involved in stalking domesticated cattle). Cats are big-time hunters. They're designed to stealthily ambush and play with their prey. When was the last time your cat licked its lips when it saw a grazing cow?

By nature, indoor felines quickly adapt to their surroundings and hunt what's available. They enjoy meals that offer a challenge and make it fun to eat; Big game that run, hide, wiggle, squirm, swim, and fly. So, next time you're at the market ask for mouse, lizard, sparrow, spider, and roach. Your cats will thank you.

The Cats' Meow! **Meaty Mice** *In Sauce* NET WT. 5.5 OZ (156g)

The Cats' Meow! **Lizard Stew** *Scale Free* NET WT. 5.5 OZ (156g)

The Cats' Meow! **Savory Sparrow** *Bite Size* NET WT. 5.5 OZ (156g)

The Cats' Meow! **Sliced Goldfish** *Packed in Water* NET WT. 5.5 OZ (156g)

The Cats' Meow! **Gourmet Roach** *In Natural Juices* NET WT.

The Cats' Meow! **Spider & Fly Dinner** *Select Cuts* NET WT.

Fur in Our Food

All Southern Californians are supposed to be fit and tan. And then, there's Jerry. Because he's such an accomplished hunter, talented beggar, and hearty eater, some visitors upon first meeting Jerry have mistakenly asked, "When are her kittens due?" Well, there's a lot to love about him. He has California's golden glow, but he's definitely not a hard body; more a flabby tabby (a true couch cat). We call him "growl tiger" for the times when his naps are rudely interrupted. Jerry's perfectly comfortable on our lap, then we move. Obviously, he has to growl his displeasure. It's unhealthy to let things eat at you.

Jerry's girth snuck up on us. We've read that a cat's whiskers are their curb feelers: If the whiskers fit through an opening, then the cat will too. Unfortunately for Jerry, it's not true. While documenting our Cats' House for Japanese television, a crew member suggested that Jerry pass through our hallway's star-shaped opening. He resisted at first, so I pushed him. His whiskers went through easily. But, the rest of him became hopelessly stuck! Jerry's feet flailed in all directions. We laughed hysterically. He growled. And, the cameraman kept filming. We hadn't realized that our biggest eaters had outgrown some of their catwalk openings. Now: Jerry, Bernard, and Denise are unhappily on diets.

Fur in Our Food

P a r t y A n i m a l

After-dinner treat, anyone?

I'm dull, and Frances is even duller. When we want to have a good time, we stay home and watch our cats. Our intoxicating substances are usually tea and soda pop. But, that's not true of our cats, who've been known to indulge in a certain weed.

Life's good, but we're worried. Within a mile of our house, recreational catnip is for sale at our grocery store. And now, higher potency, designer catnip is available to anyone over the Internet. We understand that cats need to let their fur down occasionally, but bite the hand that feeds you?

The Calm After the Meal

We've all seen the pictures of roaring lions with their jaws ferociously open. Scary. But, big cats are not always what they seem. That oversized tabby is probably yawning after a satisfying meal, getting ready for the next nap. Our little lions need rest too—up to sixteen hours a day for the average feline. Their mealtime sequence is repeated three times daily—spontaneous feeding frenzy, followed by big yawns, and then, blissful tranquillity.

A **Lot** of H

It's only natural for families that have shared as many naptimes and mealtimes as we have to want to help each other. But, sometimes, the bond that we form is too close—like when our inseparable roommates are left home alone. The cats are terrific in our absence: An occasional cupboard might be opened; unprotected food discovered and joyfully eaten; or, a yarn ball (or two, or three) unraveled. But, dog Sasha hasn't been trusted since the first week she leaped into our lives, and thrashed our curtains and office door. When Frances and I left her inside, we did not realize how desperately she needed our reassurance and constant companionship. Sasha desperately clawed and clawed at the doors through which we might have abandoned her. She's probably better now, but—just in case—we still put her out when we leave. Now we know that a Siberian Husky can do more damage in a few minutes than nine felines can in several months.

Ordeal for All

Sometimes, cats are too helpful for their own good

It seems auspicious that Frances and I both fossilized in 1986, the Chinese Year of the Tiger. That's when we moved to our present location, and decided to settle down and raise our feline family. There will be no more moves for us. We want to stay here for the rest of our lives!

Now with the help of our cats we can paint walls any color that we want; modify rooms beyond recognition; and build overhead walkways just for the fun of our feline family. We'll never have to worry about losing money on the resale of our home, because we're not going to sell!

Frances is our chief colorist and painter. No task is too small for her "little helpers." Jerry's specialty is applying wide-bodied, therapeutic heat to tired laps and backs. Without his warm assistance, our lives would be less soothing.

Perhaps, Simon thought that his pink *faux fur* look was fashionable. To us, it looked like another painting misadventure. Nevertheless, it had to go. At the Cats' House, it's all for one, and one for all—bath time for everyone. Jimmy's curiosity misguided him into being the first cat in the tub.

A Lot of Help

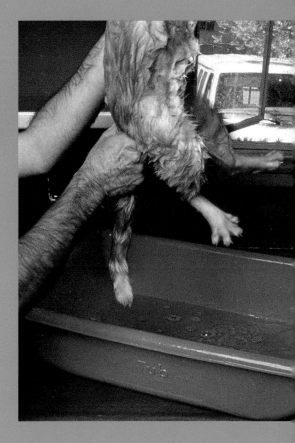

At best, baths are difficult for all concerned. For Frances and me, they're definitely a wet, two-person, four-hand job. For our bathers, it's a wet, no-holds-barred, escape-the-moment-you-can, revolting experience.

Our slippery felines may think their hateful baths can be avoided, but (so far) we've always won. Even pink-free Simon will soon be his helpful self again.

Not one of our cats believes us when we tell them, "This hurts us more than it does you." Frances and I may win the bathing battles, but we're the ones with the field injuries. In self-preservation, we now take our felines to the groomers. Sometimes, it pays to share your skirmishes with professionals.

Last Licks

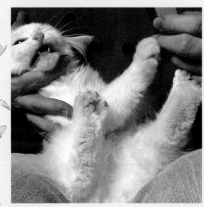

An amazing thing about cats is their willingness to forgive. You've just violated their cathood: They've been shoved into water; forcefully restrained; lathered with foul-smelling shampoo; fur-ruffled with a towel; flea-combed; toenail-clipped; and, worst of all, lied to: "Don't take this all so personally. Taking a bath isn't so bad."

How could they not take it personally? It was all done to them! But, what's even more amazing is how quickly they forgive us. Within minutes, we're buddies again, and they're purring on our in-need-of-cat laps.

Those little barbs on cats' tongues may be perfect for cleaning fur, but help is sometimes needed for hard to lick areas like the ears. That's when it's nice to have your own dog. Sasha is well suited for the task. Her tongue is soothing and large: A lot of fur can be washed quickly (but too slobbery for some cats' taste). Half of our kitties line up for Sasha's mobile ear service, while the other half question whether it's worth it. With so many choices and all of the responsibility, it is not easy being the only dog for nine cats.

Floored Felines

And Further Fun Projects

The cats are both helpers and inspiration for our remodeling projects. But, they weren't alone in needing a healthy cleanup. Our kitchen floor demanded far more than their flea shampoo and water treatment. Its only solution was to bury it from view, and start anew with a clean plywood slate. I laid the wood foundation, and left the rest for Frances to complete. She gets full credit for inexpensively transforming our beastly linoleum into feline friendly flooring.

For six months, Frances cut out and cut out lots and lots of cats from *Cat Fancy* and *Cats* magazines; as well as supplementing her collection with snips from calendars and photo books. Finally (several scissor calluses later), she was ready to prep the plywood base: filling screw holes and seams with wood putty; sanding the surface smooth; then, sealing the floor with Varathane Professional Clear Finish SB.

Just when Jimmy was comfortable in his newly discovered box, Frances rudely pulled a cat cutout from under him—disrupting his peaceful nap.

Would hundreds of flat cats improve your floor?

She then lifts the cutout from the work area while it is still wet. Frances's gluing board is a leftover piece of acrylic (glass works well too).

Frances applies Liquitex Acrylic Matte Medium to the back of her cutouts with a one-inch paintbrush (being careful to minimize the amount of glue adhering to the front).

Large, square background pictures are first applied faceup to cover wide areas quickly. Then, cutouts are placed over them to hide the harsh edges and add diversity.

Frances has impeccable taste, but her guard is down when cats are around. I've never seen a feline that she didn't immediately fall in love with and want to take home; even stuffed cats captivate her.

A plastic squeegee is used to flatten the cutouts, and remove excess glue. Finally, at least two coats of Varathane are applied with a foam roller to finish the feline floor. Caution: Cats should refrain from helping while the sealant is being applied and drying.

TomCat doesn't have the faintest idea why Frances would squash him against her stuffed cats. By going limp, maybe she'll quit this strange behavior and return him to his nap basket.

Polecats

For several months, the children in San Diego were probably not receiving stuffed cats from thrift stores, because Frances was buying every one that she could find. Our inspired plan was to erect a cat column in our TV room and cover it with, of course, stuffed cats. We figured it would provide a cushy, padded path to the catwalk. Construction went smoothly: An additional fourteen feet of catwalk was added, and ninety-three plush cats (and two mice) were attached with screws to the support column. Unfortunately, our kitties don't want to climb it. We've scented the column with catnip spray, pressed feet to the post, and achieved the same result each time—indifference, hissing, and escape. Maybe, we need to liven our complacent cats up with new, rambunctious kittens.

Our cat-free cat column

Sweaters into Afghans
Birds of a Feather: Frances, Cats, and Yarn Balls

Live with a person long enough and, eventually, you'll drive them bonkers. To the delight of our kitties, Frances has recently taken to buying sweaters from thrift stores, unraveling them, and turning their thread into yarn balls—a lot of yarn balls. Closets full of yarn balls. All of our cats love the yarn balls, and I like them too (up to a point). Thankfully, Frances has been turning the yarn balls into afghans—a lot of afghans. Closets full of afghans. . . .

Jimmy has been a crafty yarn-cat since kittenhood, helping Frances with all stages of afghan creation. He's there when the yarn is unraveled from sweaters; liberates her balls as fast as she can wind and hide them (unraveling the yarn throughout the house in decorative zigzag, crossover, and circular patterns); encourages fellow felines to assist with artistic yarn dispersion; and lends his warmth and purrs to in-progress and completed afghans.

All Cats Will Love

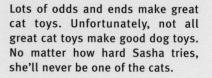

Lots of odds and ends make great cat toys. Unfortunately, not all great cat toys make good dog toys. No matter how hard Sasha tries, she'll never be one of the cats.

Cats are always there when we need assistance, but even the most energetic cat can become a dull feline without quality play-time. Ping-Pong balls and strings are two of our cats' favorite playthings. When combined, they become "String Pong"—their super action toy. It's easy to make: Drill a hole through a Ping-Pong ball; feed a string through the holes; tie knots on both sides of the ball to secure the string; and activate by dragging String Pong throughout the house. Some cats will chase the bouncing ball, and others will chase the string. You'll quickly discover which end works for your cats. (Healthy Advice: Always supervise cats around strings, and put them away when not in use. Swallowed strings can require surgical removal.)

A Lot of Help

When our cats want to play turtle, they head straight for a grocery bag. It's impossible to find hide nor hair of them (except, of course, for the exposed tail and bag wiggle). They know they're being so sneaky.

One scaredy-cat day, the handle of a shopping bag caught around TomCat's neck, setting off a frantic flight throughout the house, the bag following every movement and flapping loudly at his rear. Now, we always remove the handles.

A Lot of Help

PRIVACY
Share

We each have private sanctuaries from the others: The cats have their catwalk, Sasha has her backyard, and Frances and I have our cat-free office/work areas. Still, everyone's bone of contention is Frances's and my space. They don't understand why even helpful and loving family members can't go in there.

We love our cats and dog, but they can be attractive nuisances. They're not persuaded by the fact that picture framing is what puts the food in our bowls, and cannot be offered for napping on or claw sharpening. Our fur-producers always promise to be good. "We'll hold still and not shed." And, our reasoned response is usually, "Sorry, the answer is still: No. Why? Well, because we say so." Frances and I already share most of our private moments with them.

d

TomCat plots a way to get into the one area that's denied him.

Shower and . . .

There's no privacy in our bathroom—the cats have designated it a favorite playground. Jerry loves showers (for others), and tries to catch the falling droplets (that dribble on the opposite side of the glass door).

...Shave

We're such a close cat family that I find the need to shave regularly. Molly is my girl. She bonded to me right from the start. However, I've discovered that too much of a good thing can be a ticklish affair: Her fur sticks to my unshaven stubble and drives me crazy.

Privacy Shared

Kitty Foil

We have a black sheep in our family. Actually, Joseph is a "sweet and sour" black cat—an affectionate lap warmer with unpredictable moments of bad attitude. We still remember the day he captured the papier-mâché mermaid that was hanging on the bathroom door. Joseph leaped and dislodged the mermaid, accidentally closing the door and himself in the room. A lesser cat would have meowed for rescue; not Joseph. Now he was free to practice his toilet paper shredding without interruption. In fact, Joseph became so proficient that, in self-defense, we purchased a plastic "shred-proof" cover to foil him. Rarely do Frances and I win. Behavior modification is what happens to us after all of our efforts fail. Meanwhile, Joseph continued his shredding streak unabated until it lost its challenge; then he quit. But, we keep the plastic protector on, just in case. . . .

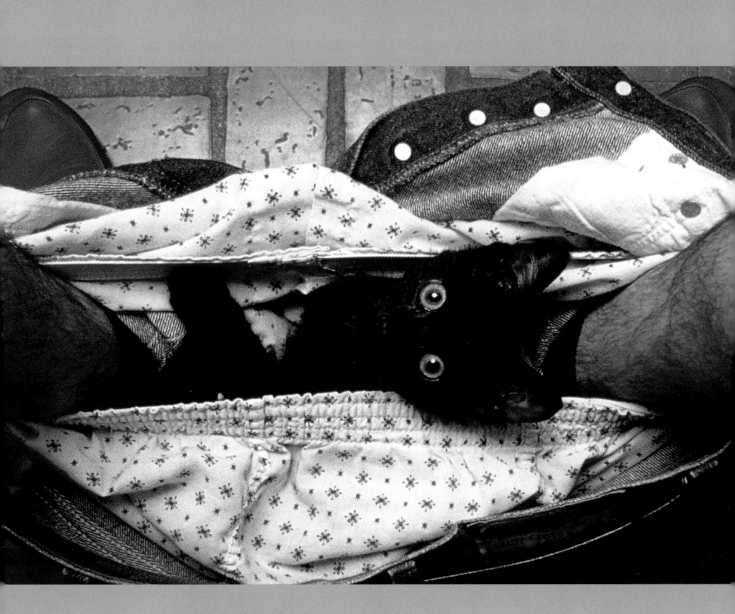

With two bathrooms and two people, it would be logical to expect one room to always be available. But, frequently our furry companions are one step ahead of us, so we share. When you live with nine cats, the unexpected should always be expected.

Tub Tabbies

When you live with a shredder like Joseph, you're guaranteed of having a constant supply of empty toilet paper rolls. Jimmy took great pleasure in swatting Joseph's rolls around the inside of our bathtub. Its steeply contoured walls form a perfect cat velodrome—frequently keeping the game pieces in play.

After Joseph quit his shredding mid-roll, we had to quickly find a substitute tub toy. Ping-Pong balls! Immediately, one cat stood out head and tail above the others: Jerry's winning attitude and terrific paw-to-eye coordination advanced him to top Tub Pong player.

Privacy Shared

TomCat:
Everyone's Favorite

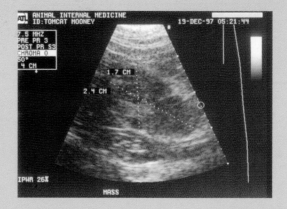

People frequently ask, "Which is your favorite?" It's impossible to select one cat over the others. They're all special in their own way. Besides, I've lost all objectivity. A good purr or endearing expression melts me in no time. However, if our visitor's opinions were counted, TomCat would win handily. When guests are available to be impressed, TomCat follows everyone from room to room and laps up the attention. He acts like a dog; so, naturally, he gets oohed and aahed more than any other cat.

Several months ago, TomCat was diagnosed with terminal, intestinal cancer, and given only six months to live. Thankfully, we noticed his symptoms early, allowing his medication to minimize his weight loss and stomach indigestion. We're hopeful, but realistic. By the time this book is in bookstores, TomCat will likely be frolicking on a much higher catwalk.

Sadly, there is an unavoidable disparity between the average life spans of cats and people. Over the years, we've had several people confide in us that they couldn't bear to have another animal companion because of the heartbreak when theirs passed away. For Frances and me, our tears and heartfelt sorrow are confirmation of our need to be touched by another. TomCat will always be one of our "favorites"—one of the sweetest kitties we've ever met; a plate licker and chicken stealer; and a reminder of how special shelter cats can be if we open ourselves to others.

Probably, the most frequently asked questions that we receive are about our least favorite cat task: "Do you use clumping or regular cat litter?" [Clumping] "How often do you clean your cat boxes; how many do you have?" [Every other day; five boxes] "Who cleans the boxes?" [Bob—males are genetically suited for litter]

"Do you have a lion?" asked the clerk, as I was paying for my three hundred pounds of generic, Slim Price cat litter. Our best source (before they closed), was a discount warehouse that repackaged grocery stores' broken litter bags. Most litter companies package a carefully filtered, consistently textured product. But, for Slim Price, all of the spilled brands were swept together to form its own surprising mixture of granularity.

In fact, our gray guy, Bernard, would race to be first to use the Slim Price litter. He would stand half in/half out, and dig and dig and dig, until he found the dog crunchies that might have inadvertently been swept into the combined litter. Unfortunately, Bernard is no longer first-cat-in-box now that we use a no-doggie-treats clumping litter.

House Rules

We love our cats, but sometimes they act like animals. To be candid, Frances and I are humans. We try, but fail to shed our speciesist baggage. Over and over we spinelessly prove that we're pushovers: Almost everything that our companions do is forgiven and forgotten.

However, unauthorized spraying is probably our biggest taboo. All of our kittens are spayed and neutered within their first six months to curb overpopulation and territorial marking. But, Simon and Joseph easily overcame all of our human hurdles. For over a year, they sprayed everything that needed to be scented. We discovered it takes more than a timely scalpel, well-aimed squirt bottle, countless spotless cleanups, or female hormone therapies to dissuade cats from acting naturally. Finally, we admitted defeat and banished them to nature's splendor—the great outdoors.

Our indoor cats watch Joseph become an outdoor cat.

Simon

Joseph

Joseph and Simon are perfectly at home outside, although Simon's curiosity almost killed him on his first day out. He trapped himself, upside down in a narrow box, for hours, on one of our year's steamiest days. Luckily, after repeated calling, I heard his barely audible, muffled meow. Now, Simon is thriving outside, and is considered quite the hunter. Joseph, on the other paw, took to the chase immediately, specializing in lizards and birds (until he was debirded with a bell attached to his collar).

We have wonderful neighbors, but several years ago on Halloween eve, an unsigned note was attached to our front door, demanding ". . . keep your (expletive) cats out of my yard and off my car. . . ." So, we did. We took Simon and Joseph to stay temporarily with Frances's parents until I could build them an outdoor enclosure. They made themselves right at home, and think Stelle (her mom) is the greatest. I still have grand visions for our outside Cat Playland (but nothing on paper). Meanwhile, the Mooneys now have two loving kitties (that spray occasionally).

Like It or Not

And,
Not a
Creature
Was
Stirrir

g...

. . . Not Even a Cat?

Bedtime at the Cats' House is a moving experience. But, don't tell that to the manufacturer of our electric blanket. Its warranty coverage excludes our nightly cat coverage. The "Do's and Don'ts" categorically forbid pets from setting paw or fur on top of the blanket (as if we could stop them). Apparently, our heat-seekers could break the blanket's fragile wiring, or worse, make it overheat from their additional warmth sandwiching us from above. For years, I was fearful that the manufacturer might discover our nightly violation. Thankfully, we've enjoyed more than twenty years of trouble-free sleeping—and are safe from spontaneous cat combustion.

It didn't take as long to get over the fear of moving my legs. They would cramp before I would shift and disturb a peaceful catnap. "Let sleeping cats lie," I used to say. Now, it's every cat and person for themselves. I'm able to toss and turn all night long—completely guilt free.

What happens when the lights go out? To find out, we mounted a motorized camera to the ceiling directly over our bed. For over a week, in total darkness, a powerful flash illuminated our bed every thirteen minutes throughout each night. After a couple of evenings, everybody slept comfortably.

An animated slide show of *A Typical Night* can be viewed on the Internet at www.thecatshouse.com.

A Typical Night

And, Not a Creature Was Stirring . . .

And, Not a Creature Was Stirring . . .

And, Not a Creature Was Stirring . . .

Our nightly rest is not assured until Sasha has had her two-in-the-morning walk. We must offer a startling vision for early drivers; especially the sight of Frances outfitted for the cool air in her ear-warming cat hat.

It is often said that by opening our heart to the needs of others, our own life will be changed as well. In Frances's case, her unabiding love for cats has literally gone to her head. Now, if we could only know what our fur-companions think of this half-feline/half-feeder creature?

Last Dance

My feet never made the right moves, but there's always hope that I'll learn to dance. I'm still weighted by baggage from my formative years (plus some additional girth from later years). Thankfully, Frances helped me overcome one of my worst holdovers: "Felis deprivation." Until we were married, I had only experienced the pleasure of living with one feline. Now, (thanks to Frances) we have nine at one time!

Curiously, nine feels quite normal—like Frances and I were supposed to enjoy fur-filled living in our prime years. Unfortunately, movies oftentimes give a scary picture of people like us: Deranged spinsters are shown with cats swarming over every surface and underfoot. Luckily, our cats are frequently overhead (freeing our surfaces), and rarely under our feet. As far as we can tell, we're not Hollywood material yet.

In fact, at this point in our relationship, we're more romance novel than scary movie. Frances and I have been married now for twenty-five years, and have had the good fortune to live and work at home with our feline (and dog) family for the past six years. From food input to output, work to play, waking moments to counting cats in our sleep . . . our family's nonstop togetherness has truly made our lives inseparable.

Without warning, however, we discover that our time together is limited. Typically, felines' life spans are only one-seventh as long as they are for their feeders. With much sadness, we're forced to accept the loss of our loved ones. It is our hope that *Cats into Everything* will encourage others to look into their own relationships (animal and human), and devote more "quality" time before it's too late. TomCat would love that.

Acknowledgments

Frances and Estelle Mooney's steadfast support, faith, wit, inspiration, sustenance, sacrifice, and creativity made my efforts possible. Cats into Everything *is dedicated to them; and, in loving memory of Jack and Nancy Mooney.*

It's supposed to get easier the second time around. And, it was for much of *Cats into Everything*, my sophomore authorial effort. However, before my first book, *The Cats' House*, was a publisher proposal, I had the luxury of slowly transforming and revising it as many times as my inexperience necessitated. So, I did: *The Cats' House* turtled its way from concept to completion in a leisurely eight years. *Cats into Everything* is a different story: Total personal immersion, and finished in a feline-fast nine months! Luckily, many of the book's photos were already in my portfolio. Otherwise, I would still be turtling along. . . .

To be honest, creating an illustrated book like *Cats into Everything* is a lot of work (and a labor of love). Andrews McMeel Publishing, Kathy Viele (ace cat editor), Carol Coe, Michelle Daniel, Norma Groom, Katie Mace, and Eden Thorne are a dream team to work with.

A surprisingly diverse family of supporters helped make this book possible. *Thank you!*

Every author's fantasy is to be granted the trust and artistic freedom that I've fortunately received on my first two books. Thankfully, Andrews McMeel encouraged me to wear several creative hats, donning headgear as the book's photographer, writer, and designer. With sincere appreciation, thank you for giving me the opportunity to succeed (or fail). I've tried to create a book that we could all be proud of.

Quite simply, *Cats into Everything* would not have been possible without the assistance, encouragement, collaborative skills, and guidance that countless individuals provided. In advance, I apologize for any unintentional omissions.

Thank you for making *Cats into Everything* possible: James Ard; Lee Austin; Tyler Blik; Shannon Carroll; Amy Shojai and Sally Bahner, Cat Writers' Association; Linda Chester, Laurie and Chloe Fox, Linda Chester Literary Agency; Dennis and Sue Reiter, Tim Bee, Sam Nakamura, Chrome Film and Digital Services; David Covey; Kay and Margie Crosbie; Tim and Sherry Crump; Dennis, Barbara, Christine, Andrew, and Jenny Culleton; Dick and Red Culleton; Omer Divers; Charles, Annie, and Sydnee Drake; Dr. Harold Stephens, Dr. Cheryl Clark, Kimberlee Louder, Charmain Sanchez, and Jessica Byrd, Fletcher Hills Pet Clinic; Robbie and Lesley La Fuze; Dave Garcia; Louis Goldich; Grossmont College Photo Club; John and Laura Cunningham Hilbig; Deacon Holden; Melinda Holden; Suda House; Hyde Gallery, Grossmont College; John Kalpus; Naomi Kartin; David Katz; Mario Lara; Tom Lazzara; Mary Beth Link; Edna Loeb; Douglas McClure; Dinah McNichols; Ron, Sandy, Derrick, and Brian McPherson; Wayne and Nora Miller; Katherine Mooney; John Moore; Ernie and Muriel Morrison; Barbara Murray; Gerri Calore, Denise Johnston, and dedicated staff, National Cat Protection Society; Allwyn O'Mara; Pat Rose; Carmen Rusnack; Robert Schneider; Joyce Cutler Shaw; Norman Sizemore; Carrie Soler; Paul Stamm; Bruce, Suzie, Stacey, Kimberly, and Melissa Stoll; Edith Stoll; Jan and Linda Tonnesen; Hitoshi and Terri Tsuchida; the Viele menagerie—Bonnie, Chaps, Chester, Connery, Encore, Fable, Falstaff, Kathy, Mickey, Ruby, Sam, Splash, Steve, Touché, and Woody; David Wing; Robert Ziegler; and, of course, Mom and Dad. *Thank you!*

Photo Notes/Credits: Photo-illustrations were created from multiple images composited together on pages 9, 10-11, 12, 16-17, 22-23, 32, 35, 56-57, 68, 72-73, and 90. All photographs in *Cats into Everything* are by Bob Walker, except: Picture of Frances, page 10, taken by Jack Mooney; and photo of Bob, page 11, photographer unknown.

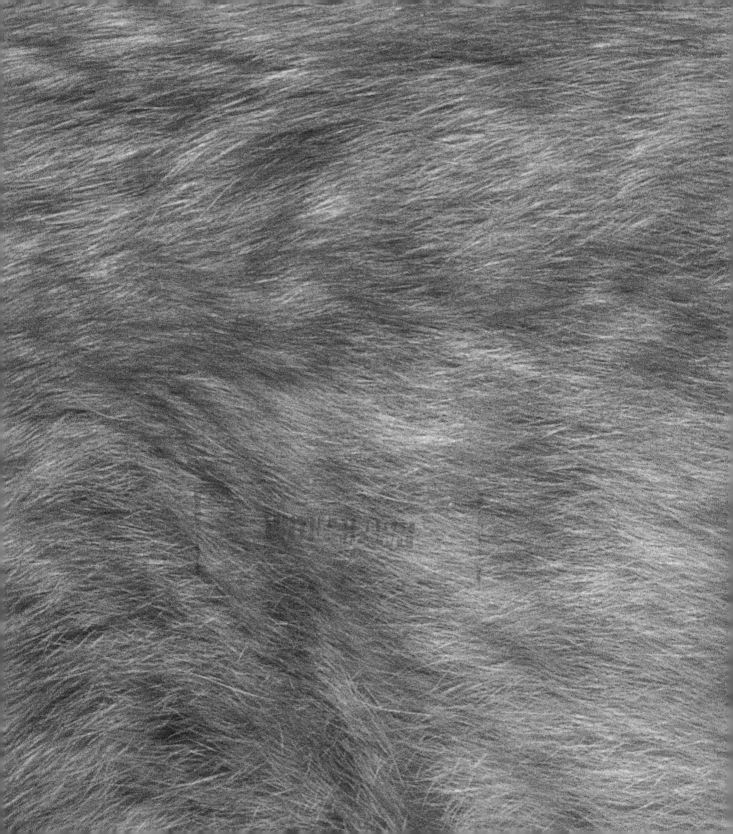